Super

FANTASTIC

STORIES

FOR CURIOUS KIDS

Astonishing Tales From the World of Science, History, Animals, Earth and Everything in Between

Gumafa Huplonu

TABLE OF CONTENTS

Introduction   1

Albert and the Magic of Curiosity   3

Storm of Destiny: The Hurricane That Shaped a Nation   6

The Challenge of Change   9

The Eternal Wanderer   13

Frozen Fury: The Blizzard That Buried New York   16

The Dance of Giants: 18

A Carnival Memory   18

Nikola's Bright Idea   22

Marla's Colorful World   26

Neil's Journey to the Stars   30

Freedom, Fries, and Foolery   34

The Kid with a Big Heart and a Bigger Swing   37

Magic in the Air   41

The Clever Octopus   44

Tara and Bella: The Unlikely Friendship   47

The Enchanted Dance   50

Adventures on Monkey Island   54

The Great Rabbit Mystery   58

The Great Eiffel Tower Scam   61

Mike, the Miraculous Headless Chicken   66

Clementine Delake: The Mermaid Girl   69

Conclusion   72

Introduction

Once there was a boy who built a rocket in his backyard...

Once there was a woman who could speak to animals in a way no one else could...

Once there was a town where it rained pancakes every morning...

Once there was a man who could walk on water, or so people thought…

Once there was a garden that grew books instead of flowers…

Once there was a magician who could pull stars out of the sky…

Once there was an island where time stood still…

Once there was a scientist who turned invisible…

The list of "Once there was..." could go on forever. That's the magic of stories—they're endless, full of wonder and curiosity, each one a doorway to a new adventure. The tales in this collection, however, are not mere fantasy. They are all true, drawn from the strange and fascinating corners of our world. Here, you will find stories that are stranger than fiction, proving that reality is often more surprising than anything we could imagine.

People have always found ways to amaze and baffle, from crafting brilliant illusions to pulling off unbelievable feats. Consider a con artist so clever he nearly sold the Eiffel Tower not once, but twice. Or the master magician who made the Statue of Liberty disappear right before an audience's eyes, leaving them speechless. If you're looking for stories that entertain and bewilder, turn the page.

This collection also reveals tales of incredible resilience and unexpected triumphs. Learn about Mike the Headless Chicken, who survived for 18 months without a head, confounding scientists and capturing the world's imagination. Or the town in France where, one summer, people began to dance uncontrollably, a mysterious plague that doctors and priests struggled to understand. If you're seeking stories of perseverance and mystery, keep reading.

The animal kingdom has its share of marvels as well. Discover the story of a monkey that loved to play pranks on tourists, becoming a legend on its island. Or read about an octopus with an uncanny ability to solve puzzles and escape from any enclosure, outsmarting even the cleverest of humans. If you're curious about the incredible talents of animals, read on.

Places, too, have their secrets. There's the tale of a village haunted by strange hallucinations that caused an entire community to see things that weren't there. And then there's the story of a hurricane that set a young boy on a path to greatness, leading him to become the first human to walk on the moon. If you're eager to explore the world's most mysterious and surprising locations, dive into these pages.

And there are stories that simply defy belief—a girl who painted like a seasoned artist before she could even spell her name, a magical friendship between a dog and an elephant that captured the hearts of everyone, or a monkey who was believed to be cursed, feared, and revered all at once. If you're ready to be amazed by the truly inexplicable, your adventure starts here.

Within these pages, you'll find humor, mystery, adventure, and a touch of the bizarre. You'll meet people at their most ingenious, animals that surprise and delight, and places that seem too extraordinary to be real. Read on to discover the astonishing truths and delightful oddities that make our world so wonderfully strange.

Albert and the Magic of Curiosity

Young Albert Einstein sat on the steps of his house, watching the world around him. He was only ten years old, but he already had a deep curiosity about how things worked. While other kids played games and ran around, Albert was lost in thought, staring at the sunlight dancing through the leaves of a tree.

"Albert, what are you thinking about?" his mother asked, stepping outside with a basket of laundry.

Albert looked up, his face serious. "I'm thinking about light, Mama. Why does it move so fast? And why does it make shadows like this?" He pointed to the shadows on the ground, shifting as the leaves swayed in the breeze.

His mother smiled. "You always have such interesting questions, Albert. Maybe one day you'll find the answers."

Albert nodded. He wasn't sure how, but he knew he wanted to understand the mysteries of the world. Every day after school, he would sit and think or read books that were far beyond his grade level. He loved math and science the most. Numbers and formulas seemed like a secret language that could explain everything around him.

One day, Albert's father gave him a gift that would change his life forever: a simple compass. Albert's eyes widened as he held it in his hands. "What is this, Papa?" he asked.

"It's a compass," his father explained. "It helps you find your way by pointing north, no matter where you are."

Albert turned the compass around in his hand, watching the needle move. No matter how he turned it, the needle always pointed in the same direction. "But why does it do that?" he asked, his curiosity growing even more.

His father shrugged. "That's just how it works, Albert. It's something called magnetism."

Albert was fascinated. He spent hours staring at the compass, wondering how the invisible force could move the needle. He tried to imagine the force around him, pulling on the needle, but he couldn't see or feel it. This idea that something invisible could have such a strong effect on the world amazed him.

That night, Albert lay in bed, thinking about the compass and the invisible forces around us. "If magnetism is real, what other invisible forces are there?" he wondered. "How do they work? How do they shape the world?"

Albert decided he wanted to learn everything he could about these forces. He read every book he could find on science and math. He asked his teachers endless questions, always wanting to know more. Some of his teachers thought he was strange because he was so focused on things other kids didn't seem to care about. But Albert didn't mind. He loved learning and felt that the world was full of mysteries waiting to be solved.

As he grew older, Albert's curiosity didn't fade. It grew stronger. He began to study how light travels, how gravity works, and why time seems to move the way it does. He would often sit quietly, just thinking, imagining himself riding on a beam of light through the universe.

One day, his teacher asked, "Albert, why do you always ask such strange questions? Why can't you just learn what's in the books like everyone else?"

Albert smiled. "Because I want to understand the world, not just know about it. I want to know why things are the way they are."

The teacher nodded thoughtfully. "Well, keep asking your questions, Albert. Sometimes, the people who ask the strangest questions find the most important answers."

And Albert did. He grew up to become one of the greatest scientists of all time. He discovered many things about the universe that no one else had thought about. He figured out how gravity works and why time is different for everyone, depending on how fast they are moving. His ideas changed the world forever.

But no matter how much he learned, Albert always kept his childlike curiosity. He believed that asking questions was the key to discovering new things. He once said, "The important thing is not to stop questioning. Curiosity has its own reason for existing."

Storm of Destiny: The Hurricane That Shaped a Nation

Alexander Hamilton trudged through the pouring rain, feeling the weight of the day's work pressing heavily on him. At Kortright and Cruger's trading firm, he had been managing things well since Mr. Cruger fell ill and sailed away last year, leaving him in charge. The traders appreciated his diligence, but Alexander yearned for something more significant than tallying flour and counting bills.

The wind picked up as he made his way home, pushing him forward with increasing intensity. He hoped Sarah had remembered to secure the window; his cherished books were at risk of being ruined.

As he entered the house, Mrs. Stevens greeted him with urgency. "Alexander, you're finally here! I need more firewood for the hearth."

"It's good to see you too, Mrs. Stevens," Alexander replied, though the exhaustion in his voice was evident.

"What was that?" she asked.

"Nothing," he mumbled, heading back out into the storm. He grabbed a stack of sodden wood, the rain turning it even more unmanageable.

"This wood is soaked!" Mrs. Stevens complained as Alexander returned, struggling with the wet logs.

"It's raining heavily," Alexander said. "It's not possible to find dry wood in this downpour."

"Enough of your sass, young man!" Mrs. Stevens scolded, brandishing a wooden spoon.

"Anna," Mr. Stevens said without looking up from his papers, "let the boy be."

A fierce gust of wind made them all turn to the window. "This is more than a mere squall," Mr. Stevens murmured. "It's a hurricane."

The wind howled as if in fury, and lightning split the sky, illuminating the chaotic scene outside. Trees bent like grass under the storm's force, and a massive branch crashed into a nearby house. Sarah gasped, and another branch flew past their window, cracking the glass. The storm's roar grew deafening.

The family huddled together, helpless, as the fire sputtered out and their dinner was abandoned. The tempest raged on, its ferocity overwhelming. Alexander stared through the fractured window, fear gripping him as he wondered if their home would withstand the storm.

Time seemed to stretch endlessly until, abruptly, the storm ceased. After a cautious wait,

Alexander and Mr. Stevens lit a lantern and ventured outside. The world was eerily silent, but the oppressive humidity lingered, a reminder of the storm's recent rage. Their home stood largely intact, a small relief amidst the devastation.

The cellar, however, was blocked by debris from a collapsed roof. As Alexander and Mr. Stevens struggled to clear it, the wind picked up once more, and rain began to pour again. They hurried back inside, enduring yet another endless stretch of fear and noise.

Somehow, Alexander fell into a restless sleep. When he awoke, daylight streamed through the cracked window, revealing the extent of the damage. The town of St. Croix lay in ruins—houses flattened, people injured and exposed, and the town itself appeared as if it had been trampled by a giant in a fit of rage.

Alexander observed his town's desperate attempts to rebuild. About a week later, he wrote to his father:

"I pen this letter to give you an imperfect account of one of the most devastating hurricanes ever recorded. The destruction wrought upon our town is beyond words."

This letter was published in the local newspaper, capturing the attention of readers who were amazed by Alexander's eloquence and insight. Recognizing his potential, they supported his move to New York for further education.

In 1772, Alexander Hamilton went to New York, where he received the education that would shape his future. He fought in the Revolutionary War, became the first Secretary of the Treasury, and played a pivotal role in establishing the financial system of the United States. All this began with a powerful letter describing the hurricane that reshaped his town.

The Challenge of Change

The final bell rang, sending a rush of students into the hallways of Laney High School. Michael gathered his books slowly, trying to keep his nerves in check. This was the day he had been waiting for, the day that would tell him if all his hard work had paid off. He slung his bag over his shoulder and made his way toward the gym, where the bulletin board hung, ready to reveal the results.

Michael had spent countless hours on the court, pushing himself harder than ever before. His jump shot had improved, his defense was tighter, and he felt more confident handling the ball. But now, as he walked down the hallway, doubt began to creep in. What if it wasn't enough?

When he reached the gym, a group of students was already gathered around the bulletin board. Michael's heart pounded in his chest as he pushed through the crowd. He didn't bother with the varsity list. Instead, he looked straight at the paper labeled "Junior Varsity." His eyes scanned the names, and there it was—Michael Jordan.

He should have felt relief, but instead, a mix of emotions swirled inside him. He had made the team, but it wasn't the team he had wanted. Michael stepped back, letting other students take his place at the board. He walked slowly out of the gym, his mind racing. He had worked so hard, and yet, here he was, not quite where he had hoped to be.

"Michael!" a voice called out. He turned to see his friend Larry jogging toward him, grinning. "I saw your name on the list! We're both on JV! Isn't that great?"

Michael forced a smile. "Yeah, it's good," he said, but his heart wasn't in it. Larry didn't notice, too excited about making the team to see the disappointment in Michael's eyes.

As they walked together toward their lockers, Larry talked nonstop about the upcoming season, the games, and how they were going to prove themselves. Michael nodded along, but his thoughts were elsewhere. He knew that being on the junior varsity team was an achievement, but it felt like a step back from what he had dreamed of.

When Michael got home, he found his mother in the kitchen, preparing dinner. She looked up and smiled. "Hey there, how was your day?"

Michael dropped his bag by the door and shrugged. "I made the JV team," he said, his voice flat.

His mother wiped her hands on a towel and came over to him. "That's great, Michael! I'm proud of you."

"Yeah, but it's not varsity," Michael replied, frustration creeping into his voice. "I worked so hard, Mom. I thought I'd at least have a shot at making varsity."

His mother placed a hand on his shoulder, her eyes full of understanding. "I know it's not what you wanted, but this isn't the end. It's just the beginning. You're still on the team, and that means you have another opportunity to grow, to improve, and to show them what you're really made of."

Michael sighed, leaning against the counter. "But it feels like I'm not good enough."

His mother shook her head. "That's not true, Michael. You have the talent, but sometimes it takes time to get where you want to be. This is your chance to refine your skills, to work even harder, and to prove to yourself that you belong on that varsity team. Every great player had to start somewhere."

Michael nodded, a small spark of determination igniting inside him. "I guess you're right."

"Of course, I am," his mother said with a smile. "And remember, there's no shame in starting on JV. It's a stepping stone, not a setback."

Over the next few weeks, Michael dedicated himself to the junior varsity team. He practiced relentlessly, often staying late after practice to work on his shooting and ball-handling. Coach Herring noticed his dedication and started giving him more responsibilities on the court. Michael found himself leading his team, directing plays, and pushing his teammates to improve alongside him.

As the season progressed, Michael's skills sharpened. He became known for his quick reflexes, his ability to read the game, and his relentless drive. He wasn't just playing basketball—he was living it.

Then, halfway through the season, something unexpected happened. One of the varsity players got injured, and Coach Herring needed someone to step up. He called

Michael into his office after practice.

"Michael, I've been watching you," Coach Herring said, leaning back in his chair. "You've shown a lot of growth, and I think you're ready for a bigger challenge. How would you like to join the varsity team?"

Michael's heart skipped a beat. "Really, Coach? You think I'm ready?"

Coach Herring nodded. "I do. You've earned this, Michael. But it's not going to be easy. You'll have to work even harder to keep up with the older guys. Are you up for it?"

Michael nodded, determination blazing in his eyes. "Yes, Coach. I'm ready."

That evening, Michael went home with a renewed sense of purpose. He told his mother the news, and she smiled, pride shining in her eyes. "I knew you could do it," she said, hugging him tightly.

Michael stepped onto the varsity court with the same determination that had driven him all season. He knew this was just the beginning of his journey, and he was ready to take on whatever challenges came his way. He wasn't just playing for the team anymore—he was playing for himself, to prove that he could rise to any occasion.

Years later, after becoming a college star and being drafted by the Chicago Bulls, Michael Jordan would look back on that season as the turning point. It was the time when he learned that success didn't come easily, but through hard work, perseverance, and the willingness to embrace every challenge. And that lesson would carry him to the heights of greatness.

The Eternal Wanderer

"Have you noticed how slow Petunia has become lately?" Bella asked her fellow sea anemone, Oliver. "She hasn't moved an inch in days."

"Oh, I saw that," Oliver replied. "She bumped into a rock and got a bunch of her tentacles tangled up. She's reverted back to her polyp stage."

Bella sighed. "I wish everyone wouldn't keep turning back into polyps. It's so dull when they do. They just stay rooted and never want to explore."

"Well," said Oliver, "they can't really do much once they're attached to the seabed."

Bella scowled. "Sometimes I think I might need to become a polyp just to escape this monotony."

"You're still pretty young, aren't you?"

"I'm only a year old. I've been a polyp twice already."

Oliver chuckled. "Just wait until you've been through it a few hundred times. Then you might see things differently."

In the 1990s, marine biologists Sara Williams and Anton Lemaire were studying a fascinating sea anemone known as Metridium senile. Due to a minor oversight in their care routine, the anemones seemed to lose their vitality and shrunk down, becoming small, sessile blobs. They retracted their tentacles and significantly reduced in size.

As the scientists continued to observe, they discovered that these anemones had reverted to an earlier stage of their life cycle, the polyp stage. Essentially, they had become younger. Instead of perishing, Metridium senile could rejuvenate themselves by transforming back into polyps. They would then grow into fully mature anemones, resembling the adults they once were. Some likened this process to a phoenix rising from its ashes, a cycle of renewal rather than death. The sea anemone earned the nickname "the eternal wanderer."

These anemones are relatively small, about the size of a fingernail. The process by which they revert to a younger stage is known as cellular reprogramming, where cells transform into different types. This phenomenon is quite rare, but scientists are intrigued by its potential for medical advancements in humans.

The researchers have yet to find an end to their cycle of growth and regression. Dr. Koji Tanaka, a Japanese scientist, has been observing these anemones since the early 2000s and noted that some individuals have reverted to polyps and re-grown as many as 15 times within a single year.

It's important to note that no one has observed this process in natural settings, possibly due to the difficulty of spotting such small, translucent creatures in the vast ocean. Laboratory environments offer the best chance for study.

Scientists believe these anemones originated in the North Atlantic but have since spread to various oceans worldwide. Some speculate they hitch rides on drifting objects or ship hulls. After all, with eternal youth, reaching new places is not a challenge.

However, Metridium senile is not entirely invincible. Like other small marine creatures, they face predation from larger animals and are susceptible to infections. They can only achieve their immortality in protected environments.

"Watch out!" Bella shouted as she darted away from a passing predator. She glanced back and saw the predator swimming off, contentedly feeding. She couldn't find Oliver. As she continued to navigate the waters, something jostled her from behind.

"Careful," a passing shrimp said, scurrying away.

Bella felt her tentacles throb with damage. She sighed and began to sink to the ocean floor. Slowly, she retracted her tentacles and shrank in size, becoming a tiny, gelatinous blob resting on the seabed. She rested, transforming once more into a polyp.

Frozen Fury: The Blizzard That Buried New York

It was a cold day in March 1888 in New York City, a day like any other. The streets were bustling with activity. People hurried along the sidewalks, bundled in coats and scarves. Streetcars clattered down the tracks, their bells ringing through the crisp air. A shopkeeper swept the sidewalk in front of his store, his breath visible in the chill. Children played a game of stickball in an alley, their shouts echoing between the brick buildings.

"What a cold day!" said Billy, pulling his scarf tighter around his neck.

"Not as cold as last week," replied his friend Tommy. "Remember how the river almost froze over?"

Billy nodded, glancing up at the sky. "Looks like snow," he said. "But that's nothing new around here."

"What are you staring at, Maggie?" Tommy asked. Their friend Maggie was looking up at the darkening sky, her face a mix of wonder and concern.

"The clouds," Maggie said softly. "They're so heavy and dark. I've never seen them like this before."

"Oh, it's just a bit of snow," said Billy dismissively. "We've had snow all winter. What's the big deal?"

As if to answer, the wind picked up, howling through the narrow streets. The children shivered and huddled closer together. Then, without warning, the first snowflakes began to fall. At first, it was just a few gentle flakes, but soon the air was thick with swirling snow. The wind grew stronger, blowing the snow sideways and making it difficult to see.

Within an hour, the city was in chaos. The snow came down in a blinding fury, piling up in huge drifts. Streetcars were stuck on the tracks, their wheels spinning uselessly. Horses struggled to pull their loads through the growing snowbanks, their breaths steaming in the frigid air. People fought to make their way through the streets, their heads down against the driving snow.

The shopkeeper who had been sweeping the sidewalk was now trapped inside his store, the snow piled high against the door. The children, who had been playing stickball, were now huddled in a doorway, trying to keep warm. A group of workers took refuge in a nearby warehouse, huddling together for warmth as the blizzard raged outside.

The Great Blizzard of 1888 had arrived with a vengeance. The storm would last for three days, dumping over fifty inches of snow on the city and bringing it to a standstill. Trains were buried under snowdrifts, and telegraph lines were knocked down, cutting off communication with the outside world. People were trapped in their homes and businesses, unable to get out.

The snow was so deep and the drifts so high that even the tallest buildings seemed to disappear. It took days for the city to start digging out, with residents banding together to clear the streets. Men, women, and children worked side by side, shoveling snow and helping to dig out the trapped and stranded.

By the time the storm ended, it had taken the lives of over 200 people and caused untold damage. Yet, in the aftermath, the people of New York showed their resilience and determination. They came together to clear the snow, rebuild, and help each other recover.

For years after, those who lived through the Great Blizzard of 1888 would tell their stories of the storm that brought the city to its knees. And on cold, snowy days, they could still feel the chill of that long-ago blizzard and remember the strength of a city that refused to be beaten by the weather.

The Dance of Giants:
A Carnival Memory

"Papa, will we see the giants this year?" Marco asked, bouncing excitedly on the balls of his feet. His wide brown eyes gleamed with anticipation, reflecting the bright colors of the banners fluttering above the crowded square.

"Yes, Marco," his father replied with a chuckle, patting his son's head affectionately. "They'll be along soon, and you'll get a good look at them. Just be patient."

Marco tried his best to stand still, but it was impossible. The Carnival of Olinda was in full swing, and the energy of the celebration was contagious. Samba music filled the air, the beats so lively that even the colonial-era buildings, with their vibrant facades, seemed to dance along. Colorful confetti floated down like rain, settling in Marco's tousled hair and sticking to his clothes.

This carnival wasn't just any celebration. It was one of Brazil's oldest, dating back to the 16th century when the Portuguese settlers brought their pre-Lenten festivities to the New World. Over the centuries, these celebrations had evolved, blending with African and Indigenous cultures to create a unique and colorful spectacle that drew people from all over the country.

A loud cheer erupted from the crowd, and Marco craned his neck to see what was happening. Down the narrow cobblestone street, originally laid by the first settlers, towering figures began to appear, swaying gently as they made their way through the throng of people.

"There they are!" Marco shouted, pointing. "The giants!"

Indeed, the towering papier-mâché figures, known as "Bonecos Gigantes," were making their grand entrance, each one representing a different character from Brazilian folklore. The tradition of these giant puppets dates back to the early 20th century when a local artist named Mestre Vitalino first crafted them to add more flair to the carnival. Over the years, they became an iconic part of Olinda's celebrations.

There was the fearsome Zé Pereira, a character who symbolized the spirit of the carnival with his mischievous grin and rowdy nature. His presence in the parade was a tribute to the ancient tradition of "Zé Pereira" drummers who would announce the start of the carnival. Alongside him was the elegant Lady of the Night, her long gown trailing behind her, embodying the mystique and allure of the carnival nights.

As the giants approached, Marco felt a thrill of excitement mixed with a tinge of nervousness. They were much bigger up close, their oversized heads bobbing above the crowd like sentinels of a forgotten age. These figures were not just puppets but living symbols of the region's history and cultural heritage. The people around him were cheering and clapping, some even dancing alongside the giants, continuing a tradition that had been passed down through generations.

"Papa, can I take a picture?" Marco asked eagerly. "I want to show Mama how close we got!"

His father smiled but shook his head. "Not today, Marco. It's too crowded, and I don't want you to lose the phone in all this chaos."

"But, Papa!" Marco protested, his face falling.

"Next time," his father promised, pulling Marco a little closer. "Let's just enjoy the moment, alright? You'll remember this for a long time."

Reluctantly, Marco nodded, but his disappointment was short-lived. One of the giants, a jester with a bright green suit and a comically large nose, bent down low as he passed by, giving Marco a playful wink. This jester was a nod to the ancient tradition of jesters who entertained European courts, a reminder of how the old world's customs had blended with the new to create something entirely unique in Olinda. Marco burst into laughter, his earlier disappointment forgotten.

The parade continued, and Marco watched in awe as dancers in elaborate costumes twirled and spun, their movements a blur of color and rhythm. The costumes reflected the rich history of the region, with some representing the Indigenous tribes who once inhabited the land, and others echoing the opulence of the colonial era. The music grew louder, and the crowd's cheers reached a fever pitch as the last of the giants passed by, signaling the end of the parade.

As the giants disappeared down the street, Marco's father knelt down beside him. "See, Marco? Sometimes it's better to experience things without worrying about pictures. Now you have a memory that's all yours."

Marco smiled up at his father, the excitement still buzzing in his veins. "You're right, Papa. I'll never forget this."

Together, they made their way back through the bustling square, the sounds of the carnival fading into the distance. But for Marco, the images of the giants, the echoes of samba drums, and the joy of the celebration would remain with him forever, a cherished memory of a day spent with his father.

And as they walked home, passing under the colorful banners that told stories of centuries past, Marco couldn't help but wonder what adventures awaited them at next year's carnival.

Nikola's Bright Idea

Nikola Tesla was a curious boy who loved to explore the world around him. He grew up in a small village in what is now Croatia, and he was always full of questions. "Why do the stars twinkle at night?" he would ask his mother. Or, "How does the wind move the trees?" But his favorite question of all was, "How does electricity work?"

One day, young Nikola was playing in the fields near his home when he noticed something unusual. There were tall iron fences surrounding some of the pastures, and the sun was shining brightly. As he walked past, he reached out and touched the fence.

Zap! He felt a small shock run through his hand.

"Ow!" Nikola yelped, quickly pulling his hand back. He looked around, confused. "What was that?" he wondered out loud.

When he got home, he ran straight to his mother. "Mama, the fence shocked me today!" he exclaimed, still rubbing his hand.

His mother looked up from her knitting with a calm smile. "Did it now? Well, Nikola, that's called static electricity. It happens when the air is very dry, and there's a lot of friction. The metal fence builds up a charge, and when you touched it, it released that energy as a shock."

Nikola's eyes widened. "Electricity… in the air? That's amazing! Can we see it?"

His mother chuckled. "No, Nikola, we can't see it. It's one of those things you just have to know is there, like the wind or the warmth of the sun."

Nikola nodded slowly, his mind already racing with ideas. "I want to learn more about electricity, Mama. It's like magic!"

Years went by, and Nikola's curiosity only grew stronger. He spent hours reading books about science and experimenting with anything he could get his hands on. One evening, as he was tinkering with a small electric motor he had built, his father walked in.

"Nikola, you've been at that all day," his father said. "Don't you think it's time for a break?"

Nikola shook his head, not looking up from his work. "I'm so close, Papa. I just need to figure out how to make this motor run smoother."

His father watched him for a moment, then sighed with a smile. "All right, but don't stay up too late. Even great inventors need their sleep."

Nikola grinned. "I will, Papa. Just a little while longer."

But one thing bothered him: everyone seemed to be using the same type of electricity called direct current (DC). And DC was… well, it was okay, but it wasn't great. It didn't travel far, and it wasn't very efficient. Nikola knew there had to be a better way.

One night, while he was lying in bed, he had an idea. "What if," he thought, "instead of having electricity flow in one direction, it could change directions back and forth really fast?" He called this new idea "alternating current," or AC for short. It was a completely different way of thinking about electricity, but Nikola was convinced it could work.

The next day, he couldn't wait to start building a model to test his theory. His friend, Ivan, stopped by Nikola's workshop to see what he was up to.

"What are you doing, Nikola?" Ivan asked, peering over his shoulder.

"I'm building a new kind of motor," Nikola replied excitedly. "One that uses alternating current instead of direct current. It's going to be more powerful and travel much farther."

Ivan scratched his head. "Sounds complicated. Do you really think it'll work?"

Nikola grinned. "I have to try. You never know until you experiment!"

After many long days and sleepless nights, Nikola finally completed his model. He plugged it in, crossed his fingers, and flipped the switch. To his amazement, the little machine started humming and buzzing with life. Lights turned on, and the motor began to spin faster than anything he'd ever seen before.

"It works!" Nikola shouted with joy, dancing around his workshop. "Alternating current works!"

Ivan's eyes widened in surprise. "Wow, Nikola! You did it! This could change everything!"

But not everyone was as excited as Nikola. When he showed his invention to other scientists and inventors, some were skeptical.

"This will never work on a large scale," one inventor said dismissively. "Direct current is the only way to go."

Nikola didn't give up. He kept working on his idea, improving his designs, and showing people how AC could be used to power cities, light homes, and run machines. Finally, after many demonstrations and a lot of convincing, he got his big break. A man named George Westinghouse saw the potential in Nikola's idea and decided to help him.

One day, as they were setting up a demonstration, Westinghouse turned to Nikola and said, "You know, Nikola, not everyone sees the world the way you do. But that's what makes you special. You see possibilities where others see problems."

Nikola smiled. "Thank you, Mr. Westinghouse. I just want to make the world a brighter place."

Together, they built huge power stations and transmission lines using AC electricity. And soon, entire cities were lit up with bright, steady light thanks to Nikola's invention. People couldn't believe how far and efficiently the electricity could travel.

Years later, when Nikola looked out at the bright city lights from his window, he couldn't help but smile. All because he'd been curious about a little shock from a fence.

Marla's Colorful World

Marla sat on the living room floor, surrounded by sheets of paper, a rainbow of crayons, and a small set of watercolors her mom had given her. She was only three years old, but she was completely absorbed in her art, her little hands moving quickly as she filled each page with bold, bright colors.

Her dad, Mark, was watching her from the kitchen. He chuckled and shook his head. "She's at it again," he said to Laura, his wife, who was busy preparing dinner.

Laura glanced over and smiled. "She really loves it, doesn't she?"

Mark nodded. "She sure does. Who knows, maybe she's got a future as an artist."

After dinner, a family friend named Mike came over for a cup of coffee. As he sat down, he noticed Marla still painting in her little corner.

"Wow, look at her go," Mike said, nodding towards Marla. "She's so focused!"

Mark grinned. "Yeah, she's been like that all day. Every day, actually."

Mike walked over to the table where a pile of Marla's paintings sat. He picked one up and studied it, his brow furrowed in thought. "These are pretty cool, you know? They've got this abstract feel to them—like something you'd see in a modern art museum."

Laura laughed as she poured coffee into a mug. "Oh, come on, Mike. She's just a kid having fun with colors."

"No, I mean it," Mike insisted. "I own a little café downtown, and I've been thinking about putting up some art to liven up the place. These would be perfect. Mind if I borrow a few?"

Mark and Laura exchanged glances. They hadn't thought much about Marla's drawings beyond them being just a fun activity for her. "Sure, why not?" Mark said finally. "Take as many as you want."

A few days later, Laura's phone rang. It was Mike, and he sounded excited. "Laura, you won't believe this. Someone at the café just offered to buy one of Marla's paintings!"

Laura laughed, thinking he was joking. "Seriously? They know she's three years old, right?"

"Yeah, but they love it! They said it has this raw, authentic feel. They're asking how much you'd sell it for."

Laura paused, unsure of what to say. "Well… just tell them $100, I guess."

Mike laughed. "All right, hold on a second." There was a brief silence on the line, then he came back. "Laura, they said yes. They're writing a check right now!"

Laura's mouth fell open. "Really? They're actually buying it?"

"Yep! Looks like little Marla's got her first sale!"

When Laura told Mark, they both laughed in disbelief. Marla was just a toddler, but someone had seen something special in her art.

A few weeks later, the phone rang again. This time, it was an art dealer named Anthony Brunelli. "Hi, is this the parent of Marla Olmstead?"

Mark picked up the phone, curious. "Yes, this is her father. How can I help you?"

"I'm an art dealer, and I've seen some of Marla's work at a local café," Anthony explained. "I have to say, I'm incredibly impressed. She has a unique gift, a natural talent that's rare at any age, let alone at three years old. I'd love to discuss the possibility of showcasing her work at my gallery."

Mark was stunned. "You want to put Marla's paintings in a gallery? She's just playing with colors!"

Anthony chuckled. "I understand your surprise. But trust me, there's something extraordinary about her work. It's the freedom and joy she expresses through her colors—something most trained artists spend a lifetime trying to capture."

Mark and Laura talked it over that evening. They were both amazed by the attention Marla's paintings were getting. "I guess there's no harm in it," Laura said. "If people want to see her work, why not?"

So, they agreed to let Anthony display Marla's paintings in his gallery. The opening night was packed with people, all curious to see the work of the young artist. Marla's paintings, with their vivid colors and playful strokes, drew a lot of attention. People were amazed that a child so young could create something so compelling.

Reporters started calling, and soon Marla's story was in the newspapers. They called her a "child prodigy" and compared her to famous artists. Marla, meanwhile, didn't understand all the fuss. She was just happy to paint.

One day, a reporter came to interview her. He knelt down to her level, smiling. "Marla, how do you make your paintings look so beautiful?"

Marla shrugged, holding a paintbrush in her hand. "I just paint what makes me happy," she said simply.

Years went by, and Marla continued to paint, but she never let the fame get to her. She didn't paint to impress anyone; she painted because it was fun, because it was her way of seeing the world.

When she was fifteen, another interviewer asked her, "Do you still see yourself as a prodigy?"

Marla smiled. "No, I never really thought of myself that way. I just love to paint. That's all that matters to me."

It's not about what others see in your work; it's about finding joy in what you do and staying true to yourself.

Neil's Journey to the Stars

Neil Armstrong sat on the front porch steps, staring up at the night sky. Even at ten years old, he was fascinated by the stars, the moon, and the vastness of space. He often wondered what it would be like to fly among those stars or even walk on the moon.

His dad, Stephen Armstrong, a government auditor who often traveled for work, came out and joined him. "What's on your mind, champ?" he asked, noticing Neil's gaze fixed on the sky.

Neil shrugged. "Just thinking about the moon, Dad. Do you think people will ever go there?"

Stephen smiled. He loved how curious Neil was about the world. "Maybe one day, son. People are always trying to do things that seem impossible. Remember how we read about the Wright brothers? People thought they were crazy, but they proved everyone wrong."

Neil nodded. He loved reading about the Wright brothers and their first flight. "Yeah, I guess you're right. If they could learn to fly, maybe we could go to the moon someday."

"That's the spirit," Stephen said, patting Neil on the back. "Just keep dreaming big."

From that moment on, Neil was hooked on the idea of flying. He spent his free time reading books about airplanes and space, learning about pilots and astronauts, and building model airplanes in his room. His love for flight grew stronger each day.

One weekend, Neil's father took him to a nearby airfield in Ohio. It wasn't far from their home, and Stephen thought it would be a fun outing. The airfield was buzzing with activity, small planes taking off and landing.

"Look at all those planes!" Neil exclaimed, his eyes wide with excitement.

Stephen chuckled. "I thought you'd like this. Come on, let's go check them out up close."

They walked across the grassy field towards a row of parked planes. Neil ran his fingers over the smooth metal of a small biplane, feeling the coolness under his hand.

A pilot, noticing Neil's interest, came over with a friendly smile. "Hey there, young man. You like planes?"

Neil nodded eagerly. "Yes, sir! I want to be a pilot when I grow up. Or maybe even an astronaut!"

The pilot laughed. "Well, you've got to start somewhere. How about a ride? I've got some time before my next lesson."

Neil looked at his father, eyes shining with hope. Stephen smiled. "Go ahead, Neil. Just be sure to listen carefully and learn."

Neil climbed into the plane with the pilot. As the engine roared to life and they began to move down the runway, Neil felt a thrill of excitement. When the plane lifted off the ground, he felt his stomach flip, but in a good way. The world below grew smaller, and for the first time, Neil felt like he was touching the sky.

"This is amazing!" Neil shouted over the noise of the engine.

The pilot nodded. "There's nothing like it. Up here, you get to see the world from a whole new perspective."

Neil watched the world below, taking in every detail. He knew this was where he wanted to be. Flying wasn't just a hobby; it was a calling.

When they landed, Neil hopped out of the plane, practically bouncing with excitement. "Dad, did you see that? I flew!"

Stephen laughed. "I saw you, champ. You looked like you belonged up there."

From that day on, Neil was more determined than ever to become a pilot. He joined the local aviation club and started learning everything he could about flying. He spent weekends at the airfield, helping pilots and asking questions, eager to absorb as much knowledge as possible.

As Neil grew older, his interest in flying only deepened. He saved up money from odd jobs and, at the age of sixteen, earned his pilot's license even before he got his driver's license. He flew as often as he could, every flight a step closer to the stars.

One day, in high school, Neil's science teacher, Mr. Smith, noticed his interest. After class, he pulled Neil aside. "Neil, you've got a real passion for aviation. Have you ever thought about becoming an astronaut?"

Neil's eyes widened. "Do you really think I could?"

Mr. Smith nodded. "Absolutely. You're smart, you work hard, and you've got the curiosity and drive that NASA looks for. If that's your dream, go for it."

Neil knew he had a long road ahead, but he was determined. He studied hard, focusing on math and science, knowing that these subjects were key to his future in space. He learned about the new rockets being tested and the possibility of manned space flights. Every step of the way, he kept his eyes on the stars.

In college, Neil studied aerospace engineering, and after graduation, he joined the Navy, where he became a test pilot. He flew jets, tested new aircraft, and gained valuable experience that would one day lead him to NASA.

Years later, Neil achieved his dream. On July 20, 1969, he became the first person to set foot on the moon. As he took his famous first step and said, "That's one small step for man, one giant leap for mankind," he thought about all those nights staring at the stars, all the flights, and all the support from his family and teachers.

Neil's journey to the moon showed him that with hard work, determination, and a little bit of imagination, even the biggest dreams could come true.

Freedom, Fries, and Foolery

Have you ever fallen for an April Fool's joke that seemed so real, you couldn't help but believe it? Maybe your friend convinced you that you'd won a fake lottery, or your teacher made you think there was a surprise test. Pranks come in all shapes and sizes, but some are so convincing that they fool thousands of people. Imagine being tricked by a huge corporation—how would you feel?

That's exactly what happened in 1996 when the fast-food giant Taco Bell pulled off one of the most famous corporate April Fool's pranks ever. On April 1st, Taco Bell published full-page ads in major newspapers across the United States, including The New York Times, The Washington Post, and USA Today. The ads announced, in big bold letters, that Taco Bell had purchased the Liberty Bell, one of America's most cherished national symbols.

The ad read: "In an effort to help the national debt, Taco Bell is pleased to announce that we have purchased the Liberty Bell. It will now be called the Taco Liberty Bell and will remain in Philadelphia as a reminder of our country's debt and Taco Bell's commitment to saving it."

People were stunned. Could this be true? The Liberty Bell, a symbol of American independence, now owned by a fast-food chain? Citizens across the country were furious. The phones at the National Park Service, which oversees the Liberty Bell, started ringing off the hook. "How could you sell such an important piece of our history?" one caller demanded. "This is an outrage!" shouted another.

Even members of Congress got involved, calling the Park Service to demand answers. People were genuinely upset, not realizing it was all a joke.

Meanwhile, at Taco Bell headquarters, the marketing team was having a good laugh. They watched as the news spread and more and more people fell for the prank. They had spent about $300,000 on the ads, but the attention they received was priceless. News outlets started covering the story, and within hours, everyone was talking about the Taco Liberty Bell.

A few hours later, Taco Bell decided it was time to reveal the truth. They issued a press release stating, "The Taco Liberty Bell is not really for sale. It was a joke. The Liberty Bell will remain in its rightful place as one of our country's most historic treasures."

As people began to realize they had been duped, reactions were mixed. Some people were relieved and could appreciate the humor. "I have to admit, they got me good," laughed one caller. "I can't believe I fell for it!" Others, however, were not as amused. "I think it's in poor taste to joke about something so important to our nation's history," one person commented.

Even the White House got in on the fun. When asked about the Taco Liberty Bell prank during a press briefing, White House Press Secretary Mike McCurry joked that the Lincoln Memorial had also been sold—to Ford Motor Company—and would now be known as the Lincoln Mercury Memorial. The room erupted in laughter, and the joke was complete.

By the end of the day, Taco Bell's prank had not only fooled thousands but had also generated millions of dollars worth of free publicity. People who might never have thought about Taco Bell were suddenly craving a taco, all thanks to one clever joke.

This prank became an instant classic in the world of corporate humor. It was a perfect example of how a well-executed joke could capture the public's imagination, spark a bit of controversy, and ultimately remind everyone not to take themselves too seriously—especially on April Fool's Day.

The Kid with a Big Heart and a Bigger Swing

George Herman "Babe" Ruth wasn't always the famous baseball player everyone knows today. Once upon a time, he was just a kid with a big dream and a lot of energy.

When Babe was young, he didn't always make the best choices. In fact, he got into trouble a lot. He grew up in a small house in Baltimore, and his parents were always busy working. Babe, left to his own devices, found all sorts of ways to get into mischief. He'd skip school, sneak into theaters, and play pranks on the neighbors. His parents didn't know what to do with him.

One day, when Babe was just seven years old, his parents decided they couldn't handle his wild ways anymore. They sent him to St. Mary's Industrial School for Boys, a place where kids could learn discipline and some useful skills.

At first, Babe hated it there. He missed the freedom of the streets and his old life. "This place is like a jail!" he'd grumble to the other boys. "Why should I have to listen to these rules?" But it wasn't long before he found something at St. Mary's that he loved even more than his old tricks: baseball.

The boys at St. Mary's played baseball almost every day, and Babe quickly fell in love with the game. It was something about the way the bat felt in his hands, the sound of the ball cracking off the bat, and the thrill of running around the bases. He could feel the excitement in his bones.

Brother Matthias, one of the monks at St. Mary's, noticed Babe's enthusiasm and saw that he had a natural talent for the game. "George," he said one day, using Babe's real name, "you've got a real knack for this. You could be something special if you keep practicing."

Babe grinned. He liked the sound of that. From then on, he practiced every chance he got. He'd stay late after practice, hitting ball after ball, running the bases until his legs ached, and throwing until his arm was sore. And the more he practiced, the better he got.

But Babe was also a big kid with an even bigger appetite. He loved to eat, and he'd often sneak into the kitchen after dinner to grab an extra snack. One time, he was caught with a whole pie in his hands.

"George!" the cook shouted. "That pie was for dessert tomorrow!"

Babe just smiled his cheeky grin and shrugged. "I was just making sure it was good enough for everyone," he said with a wink. The other boys snickered behind the cook's back.

Despite his appetite for mischief and pie, Babe's talent on the baseball field was undeniable. He could hit the ball farther than any of the other boys. One day, during a game at St. Mary's, Babe hit the ball so hard it flew over the fence and out of sight.

"Wow!" Babe shouted as he watched the ball soar. "I think I hit that one all the way to New York!"

The other boys stared in amazement. "Did you see that?" one of them shouted. "He hit it clear out of the park!"

Brother Matthias laughed and patted Babe on the back. "You've got a gift, George. I think you're going to do great things one day."

As Babe grew older, his skills on the baseball field continued to improve. He started playing for a local team, and soon enough, word of his talent spread. He was signed by the Baltimore Orioles, a minor league team, and that's where he got his famous nickname, "Babe," because he was the youngest player on the team.

Babe didn't stop there. His talent and larger-than-life personality quickly caught the attention of the Boston Red Sox, and he joined their team, first as a pitcher and then as a powerful hitter. Babe's ability to hit home runs was like nothing anyone had ever seen. He became a sensation, drawing huge crowds to every game.

Then, one day, the New York Yankees made a deal to bring Babe to their team. It was with the Yankees that Babe became a legend. He smashed home run records and helped lead the Yankees to multiple championships. Fans loved him not just for his skill, but for his playful spirit and his big heart. He visited children's hospitals, gave away baseballs to fans, and always had a smile on his face.

Despite his fame, Babe never forgot where he came from or how hard he had to work to get there. He knew that with a little practice, a lot of heart, and maybe a bit of luck, anything was possible.

One day, after hitting yet another home run, a young fan asked him, "Babe, how do you hit the ball so far?"

Babe chuckled and said, "Just keep swinging, kid. Never stop swinging. And maybe sneak an extra pie or two. It never hurt me!"

The crowd laughed, and so did the young fan. They knew that Babe was someone who loved the game and had a big heart—and maybe a big appetite, too.

Magic in the Air

Tommy could hardly contain his excitement. He was holding his dad's hand tightly, his eyes wide with anticipation. They were on a boat heading to Liberty Island to see David Copperfield perform his famous magic trick. The wind was brisk, and the waves splashed against the side of the boat, but Tommy didn't care. Today, he was going to see a magic show unlike any other.

"Dad, do you think he's really going to make the Statue of Liberty disappear?" Tommy asked, his voice full of wonder.

His dad chuckled. "Well, that's what he says he's going to do. But remember, Tommy, it's all just a trick."

"But how can you make something so big disappear?" Tommy wondered, looking up at the towering statue as they approached the island.

"That's the magic of it, son," his dad replied with a wink. "Let's find out."

As they got off the boat, they joined a crowd of excited spectators gathered on the viewing platform. Tommy was bouncing on the balls of his feet, his gaze fixed on the stage set up in front of the Statue of Liberty. Two huge metal towers stood tall, and a giant curtain was hung between them, fluttering in the breeze.

The crowd was buzzing with chatter. Tommy overheard bits of conversations.

"I heard he's going to use lasers," said a man to his friend.

"Nah, it's all about mirrors," a woman replied knowingly.

Tommy turned to his dad. "Do you think he uses lasers and mirrors?"

"Maybe," his dad said with a smile. "Or maybe he has some magic up his sleeve."

Just then, the music began to play, and the crowd fell silent. A hush of anticipation spread like wildfire as David Copperfield appeared on the stage, waving to everyone. He had a confident smile and a glimmer in his eyes.

"Ladies and gentlemen," Copperfield announced, his voice booming through the speakers, "Tonight, we are going to do something that's never been done before. Tonight, we are going to make the Statue of Liberty disappear!"

The crowd erupted in cheers. Tommy felt a thrill run through him. This was it! The moment he had been waiting for.

Copperfield gestured dramatically, and the large curtain began to rise, slowly covering the statue. Tommy stood on his tiptoes, trying to see over the heads of the people in front of him.

"Can you see, Dad?" Tommy asked, bouncing with excitement.

"I can see just fine, buddy," his dad said, lifting Tommy up onto his shoulders.

Tommy's eyes were glued to the stage. The curtain was fully raised now, and the statue was completely hidden behind it. Copperfield walked to the center of the stage and held his hands up high.

"On the count of three, we will make history!" he shouted. "One… two… three!"

The curtain dropped.

Tommy's jaw dropped along with it. The statue was gone. Completely vanished. He rubbed his eyes, not quite believing what he was seeing.

"Dad! Where did it go?" Tommy gasped, looking around wildly as if the statue might have moved somewhere else.

"It's magic, Tommy," his dad said, though he sounded as surprised as everyone else. "Or a really good trick."

The crowd erupted into a mix of cheers, gasps, and applause. Some people were jumping up and down, others were scratching their heads, trying to figure out what just happened.

"Did you see that?" Tommy shouted, his face lit up with amazement. "It's really gone!"

Copperfield took a bow, soaking in the crowd's reaction. Then he held up his hands for silence again.

"But wait, ladies and gentlemen, this is not the end. Let's bring her back, shall we?"

The crowd cheered louder. Tommy could hardly believe it. Not only had Copperfield made the statue disappear, but now he was going to bring it back!

Copperfield turned towards the curtain. "Here we go! One… two… three!"

The curtain rose once more, and with another flourish, it dropped. There it was—the Statue of Liberty, standing tall as if it had never moved at all. The crowd went wild. Tommy's cheers mixed with everyone else's, his heart pounding with excitement.

"That was amazing!" Tommy exclaimed, clapping his hands. "How did he do that?"

His dad laughed. "That's the magic of it, Tommy. It's all about making you believe the impossible."

As the crowd began to disperse, Tommy couldn't stop talking about the trick. "Maybe he used a giant mirror, or—or maybe he had a big trapdoor!" he theorized, his imagination running wild.

His dad smiled down at him. "Well, I guess that's what makes a good magician, right? They make you believe in magic, even if just for a little while."

Tommy nodded, still in awe. "Yeah, I guess so. But you know what, Dad?"

"What's that, Tommy?"

"I think I'm going to figure out how he did it one day. I'm going to be a magician!"

His dad chuckled, ruffling Tommy's hair. "I bet you will, buddy. I bet you will."

As they made their way back to the boat, Tommy looked back at the Statue of Liberty one last time. Even knowing it was a trick, he couldn't help but feel that maybe, just maybe, he had seen a little bit of real magic that night.

The Clever Octopus

Deep beneath the waves, where sunlight barely reaches, lived Ollie the octopus. Ollie loved his life under the sea, but more than anything, he loved learning new things about the ocean.

One day, Ollie was practicing his camouflage when his friend Coral the crab scuttled over. "Hey, Ollie! What are you up to today?" Coral asked, her claws clicking excitedly.

Ollie shifted his color from a dark brown to a speckled green to match the seaweed nearby. "Just trying to blend in better, Coral. Did you know that I can change my color and texture to hide from predators or sneak up on prey?"

Coral raised one of her claws thoughtfully. "Yeah, I've seen you do it a lot. But how do you do that? It seems like magic!"

Ollie laughed. "It's not magic! I have special cells in my skin called chromatophores. These cells can expand and contract to show different colors. It's all controlled by my brain. And I also have muscles in my skin that change my texture to match the rocks or sand."

"Wow," Coral said, clicking her claws. "I wish I could do that! I just have to rely on my shell for protection."

Ollie grinned. "We all have our own special abilities, Coral. Like you, for example. Those claws of yours are great for digging and defending yourself!"

Coral smiled proudly. "That's true. But still, changing colors sounds so cool."

Ollie nodded. "It is! And it's not the only neat thing about me. I have three hearts, you know."

"Three hearts?" Coral exclaimed. "What do you need three hearts for?"

"Well," Ollie explained, "two of them pump blood to my gills, and the third one sends blood to the rest of my body. This helps me stay active and quick, especially when I need to get away from danger or hunt for food."

Coral looked impressed. "That's a lot of work for such a small body!"

Ollie shrugged his tentacles. "It's just how I'm built. And I have blue blood, too! It's because of a copper-based molecule called hemocyanin that helps transport oxygen in cold, low-oxygen environments. Pretty neat, huh?"

Coral giggled. "You're like a walking, talking ocean fact book, Ollie. What else can you do?"

"Well, let's see…" Ollie thought for a moment. "I can squirt ink when I'm scared! It creates a cloud that helps me escape from predators."

Coral nodded. "Yeah, I've seen you do that once when a big fish swam by. It's like your own little smoke bomb."

"Exactly!" Ollie said, puffing up with pride. "And did you know I can squeeze through spaces as small as a coin? My body doesn't have any bones, just a beak like a parrot's, so I can fit into tiny crevices to hide from predators or surprise prey."

Coral's eyes widened. "That's incredible! No wonder you're always exploring and finding new places. You can go anywhere!"

Ollie smiled. "That's the fun of being an octopus! There's always something new to discover, and I can get to places most creatures can't."

As they continued to chat, a large shadow passed overhead. Ollie and Coral both quickly hid—Ollie blending in with the sandy bottom and Coral digging into a small hole. They stayed perfectly still until the shadow moved on.

Once it was safe, Ollie slowly changed back to his usual color and peeked out. "That was close! It's good to stay alert down here."

Coral crawled out of her hole and nodded. "You're right, Ollie. There's always something lurking around. But it's a good thing you have all those special tricks."

Ollie chuckled. "Thanks, Coral. And you know, it's not just about hiding. Sometimes, it's fun to show off what I can do. Like this!"

Ollie suddenly shot out a burst of ink, creating a dark cloud in the water. He quickly swam around the cloud, coming up behind Coral.

"Boo!" Ollie exclaimed, making Coral jump.

"Ollie!" Coral laughed. "You scared me! But that was pretty impressive."

Ollie laughed, his tentacles waving with joy. "Just having a little fun, Coral. The ocean is full of surprises, and I'm here to enjoy every one of them!"

Coral grinned. "You sure are, Ollie. And I'm glad to be your friend to see it all."

With a happy heart, Ollie and Coral continued exploring the vast, mysterious ocean, always ready for the next adventure.

Tara and Bella: The Unlikely Friendship

One sunny morning at the Tennessee Elephant Sanctuary, Tara the elephant was walking around, enjoying the fresh air. She loved the wide-open spaces and the gentle rustling of the leaves in the trees. But something felt different that day. She could hear a faint barking sound coming from the other side of the field.

"Who could that be?" Tara wondered aloud, her large ears flapping with curiosity.

She followed the sound and found a small, scruffy dog sitting by the water's edge. The dog looked a little lost and very tired. Tara slowly walked over, her massive feet making soft thuds on the ground.

"Hello there," Tara greeted gently. "What's your name?"

The little dog looked up, her tail wagging slightly. "I'm Bella," she said softly. "I was abandoned, and I don't know where to go."

Tara's heart went out to Bella. She knew what it felt like to be alone. "Well, Bella, you're welcome to stay with me," Tara said kindly. "I could use a friend."

Bella's eyes lit up. "Really? You don't mind?"

"Not at all," Tara replied with a smile. "Come on, let's go explore!"

From that day on, Tara and Bella were inseparable. They would walk around the sanctuary together, Tara's long trunk gently patting Bella's back as they went. Bella loved riding on Tara's back, feeling the cool breeze rush through her fur.

One day, as they were taking a break under a big oak tree, Bella looked up at Tara. "Why are you so nice to me, Tara? Aren't elephants supposed to be friends with other elephants?"

Tara chuckled softly. "Well, Bella, sometimes friendship doesn't come from how we look or what we are. It comes from the heart. And I think we were meant to be friends."

Bella smiled. "I think so too."

The two friends did everything together. They swam in the lake, played in the mud, and even napped under the same tree. The other animals at the sanctuary thought their friendship was a bit strange, but they all loved seeing Tara and Bella so happy.

One afternoon, the sanctuary keepers, Julie and Mike, were watching Tara and Bella from a distance. "I've never seen anything like it," Julie said, shaking her head in amazement. "An elephant and a dog, best friends. It's just incredible."

Mike nodded. "It just goes to show, animals have feelings just like us. They find comfort and companionship in the most unexpected places."

As the weeks went by, Bella and Tara's bond grew even stronger. They developed their own special way of communicating. Bella would bark once for "yes" and twice for "no," while Tara would flap her ears or trumpet softly to show her emotions. They seemed to understand each other perfectly.

One day, as they were playing near the sanctuary's gate, Bella ran too quickly and accidentally hurt her leg. She yelped in pain and limped over to Tara.

Tara immediately noticed something was wrong. "Bella, are you okay?" she asked, concern filling her voice.

Bella tried to wag her tail but winced. "I think I hurt my leg," she said, her voice trembling.

Without hesitation, Tara wrapped her trunk around Bella gently and lifted her onto her back. "Don't worry, Bella. I'll take you to Julie and Mike. They'll know what to do."

Tara carefully carried Bella all the way to the sanctuary's care center. When Julie and Mike saw them coming, they rushed over. "Oh no, what happened?" Julie asked.

"I think she hurt her leg," Tara said softly, looking down at her friend.

Mike carefully took Bella off Tara's back and examined her leg. "It looks like a small sprain," he said. "Nothing too serious, but she'll need to rest for a few days."

Tara stayed by Bella's side the entire time she was recovering. She didn't go on walks or swim in the lake. She just sat beside her friend, offering her comfort and company.

Bella looked up at Tara with gratitude in her eyes. "Thank you, Tara. I don't know what I would have done without you."

Tara smiled gently. "We're friends, Bella. That's what friends do."

A few days later, Bella was back on her feet, and the two friends were off exploring again, as if nothing had happened. The other animals at the sanctuary watched in admiration. It didn't matter that Tara was an elephant and Bella was a dog. Their friendship was a reminder to everyone that sometimes the best friends come in the most unexpected shapes and sizes.

As the sun set over the sanctuary, Tara and Bella stood side by side, watching the sky turn pink and orange. Bella sighed contentedly. "I'm so glad I found you, Tara."

Tara gently patted Bella with her trunk. "And I'm glad I found you, Bella. You're my best friend."

And with that, the two friends continued their journey, side by side, into the beautiful evening.

True friendship knows no boundaries and comes from the heart, no matter how different we may seem.

The Enchanted Dance

In the bustling city of Strasbourg, the summer of 1518 was unusually hot. The cobblestone streets were filled with people trying to go about their daily lives despite the scorching sun. Children played near the fountains, seeking relief from the heat, while merchants fanned themselves as they tried to sell their goods.

One particularly hot afternoon, a crowd gathered in the main square. Whispers spread through the streets as people stopped what they were doing and rushed to see what was happening.

"Look, over there!" a young boy shouted, pointing toward the middle of the square.

In the center, Frau Troffea, a well-known and respected woman in the city, was dancing. But this wasn't any ordinary dance. She was twirling and leaping as if she couldn't stop herself. Her feet pounded against the cobblestones, her hair came loose from its bun, and sweat poured down her face.

"What's gotten into her?" a baker asked, wiping flour from his hands as he watched in disbelief.

"I don't know," replied a seamstress standing next to him, clutching her fabric tightly. "She looks like she's in some sort of trance!"

As the crowd continued to watch, Frau Troffea's dance only became more frantic. She moved with a wild energy that seemed to come from somewhere deep within her. Her feet were bruised and battered, but she kept dancing, her face a mix of exhaustion and strange joy.

"Stop, Frau Troffea!" called out a blacksmith. "You'll hurt yourself!"

But Frau Troffea didn't respond. She didn't even seem to hear him. She just kept dancing, her movements growing more erratic with each passing moment.

Days went by, and Frau Troffea continued to dance without rest. Her friends and family tried to intervene, but nothing could stop her. It was as if an invisible force had taken hold of her, compelling her to dance.

Then, something even stranger happened. One by one, other townspeople began to join her. First, it was a young girl, then an old man, then a merchant who dropped his bags and started to twirl beside them. Within a week, dozens of people were dancing uncontrollably in the square. The once quiet city was now filled with the sound of shuffling feet and the cries of people who didn't understand why they couldn't stop moving.

The city leaders grew concerned. "This must be the work of the devil!" cried a priest. "We must pray for these poor souls."

The local doctor had a different theory. "Their blood is too hot," he suggested, fanning himself with his hat. "We need to let them dance it out of their systems."

So, the city decided to encourage the dancing. They brought musicians to play lively tunes, hoping that if they danced enough, they'd eventually tire out and stop. They even built a wooden stage in the middle of the square for the dancers.

But the dancing continued. People danced until their feet were raw and bloody, until they collapsed from sheer exhaustion. And still, more joined them, as if the dancing were contagious.

Among the crowd, a young girl named Greta watched with wide eyes. She had always loved to dance, but this was different. She felt a strange pull in her chest, a desire to join them, but she held back, frightened by what she saw.

One evening, Greta's grandmother, a wise old woman who had seen many strange things in her life, pulled her aside. "Greta," she said softly, "I need you to promise me something."

"Yes, Grandmother?" Greta replied, looking up with concern.

"Promise me you won't go near the square," her grandmother said. "There's something dark at work here, something beyond our understanding."

Greta nodded, but curiosity gnawed at her. She wanted to know why people were dancing, why they couldn't stop. She decided to sneak out that night and see for herself.

As the moon rose high in the sky, Greta tiptoed out of her house and made her way to the square. The sight that greeted her was eerie. Under the pale moonlight, dozens of people danced silently, their shadows flickering on the walls around them.

Suddenly, Greta felt a chill run down her spine. She turned to see a figure standing in the shadows, watching her. It was Frau Troffea. Her eyes seemed different now, almost glowing in the darkness.

"Frau Troffea?" Greta whispered, her voice trembling.

The woman didn't speak but reached out a hand toward Greta. Despite her fear, Greta felt herself being drawn closer, her feet moving on their own.

"No," she thought, trying to resist. "I promised Grandmother."

Just then, a loud voice broke the silence. "Greta! Get away from there!"

It was Greta's grandmother, holding a lantern high. She rushed forward and grabbed Greta's hand, pulling her back.

As they stumbled away, the dancers continued their silent jig, unaware of anything around them. Greta's grandmother led her back home, her grip firm and protective.

The next day, religious leaders from the nearby villages arrived. They declared that the dancing was the result of a curse and decided to lead the dancers up a nearby mountain to a shrine of Saint Vitus. They believed that only through prayer and repentance could the dancers be freed.

As the priests prayed and placed red wooden shoes on the dancers' feet, the townspeople watched with bated breath. Slowly, one by one, the dancers began to stop. Their feet stilled, their bodies slumped in exhaustion, and the strange trance seemed to lift.

The city of Strasbourg returned to normal, but the memory of the dancing plague lingered. People whispered about it for years, wondering what had caused it and if it could happen again.

Greta never forgot that night. She often thought about the strange pull she had felt and the glowing eyes of Frau Troffea. She realized that sometimes, the most mysterious things in life have no easy answers. It was a lesson she carried with her always: to be cautious of what she didn't understand, and to always listen to the wisdom of those who had lived longer.

Sometimes, the mysteries of the past can teach us to respect what we don't understand and to value the wisdom of those who have come before us.

Adventures on Monkey Island

Momo the monkey sat on a large rock, scratching his head as he gazed at the sparkling blue water surrounding the small island. He loved his home on Monkey Island, where every day was an adventure. The island was full of trees to climb, fruits to eat, and, most importantly, tourists to play tricks on.

"Momo!" called a voice from behind a banana tree. It was Mimi, Momo's best friend. "What are you doing up there?"

"I'm thinking," Momo replied, leaping down from the rock and swinging over to Mimi on a low branch.

"Thinking about what?" Mimi asked, nibbling on a mango she had found.

"I think today's a perfect day to play a trick on the tourists," Momo said with a mischievous grin. "I saw a boat full of them arriving just now!"

"Oh, Momo," Mimi sighed, "you always want to play tricks. Remember last week when you took that lady's hat? She chased you around for hours!"

Momo laughed, "That was fun! And besides, the tourists love it. They come here to see us monkeys, after all!"

Monkey Island, officially known as Cayo Santiago, is a small island off the coast of Puerto Rico. It is home to about 1,000 rhesus monkeys. These monkeys are not native to the island; they were brought here in the 1930s for scientific research. The monkeys were released on the island to study their behavior in a natural environment. Since then, they have become a fascinating attraction for tourists from around the world.

The monkeys on the island are known for their clever tricks and playful nature. They often steal hats, sunglasses, and food from unsuspecting visitors. While this can be amusing, it's important for tourists to remember not to feed the monkeys or leave any trash behind, as it can harm the animals and disrupt their natural behavior.

Mimi shook her head, "Well, just be careful, okay? We don't want to scare them too much."

"Don't worry," Momo assured her. "I just want to have a little fun."

As Momo and Mimi swung through the trees, they spotted a group of tourists gathering on the beach. Momo's eyes lit up with excitement. He quickly climbed down and sneaked up behind a couple who were taking pictures.

With a swift motion, Momo snatched a shiny object from the woman's bag. It was a pair of sunglasses! He dashed away, holding them up like a trophy. The tourists gasped in surprise, and the woman chased after Momo, laughing.

"Come back here, you cheeky monkey!" she called, her voice filled with amusement.

Mimi watched from a distance, shaking her head with a smile. "Momo will never learn," she thought.

Momo ran through the trees, dodging branches and leaping over rocks, until he found a high perch. He put the sunglasses on his face and made funny faces at the tourists below. The crowd burst into laughter, and even the woman who had lost her sunglasses couldn't help but giggle.

Back on the ground, Momo carefully climbed down and returned the sunglasses to the woman, who gave him a friendly pat on the head. "You're a naughty one, aren't you?" she said with a smile.

Momo chattered happily in response, enjoying the attention. But suddenly, his ears perked up. He heard a loud noise coming from the other side of the island.

"What was that?" Momo wondered aloud.

Mimi swung over to him. "Sounds like trouble. Let's go check it out."

The two monkeys quickly made their way through the dense jungle. As they reached the other side, they saw a group of tourists trying to feed the monkeys snacks and chips from their bags.

"Oh no," Mimi said, "they don't know that it's bad for us!"

Momo frowned. "We have to do something!"

Without a second thought, Momo ran towards the tourists, waving his arms and chattering loudly to get their attention. Mimi joined in, helping to shoo away the other monkeys who were getting too close to the food.

One of the tour guides noticed what was happening and quickly intervened. "Please don't feed the monkeys," she called out to the group. "It's not good for them, and it can make them sick."

The tourists, realizing their mistake, put the food away and apologized. Momo and Mimi relaxed, feeling relieved that the situation was under control.

"Thank you, little monkeys," the guide said with a smile, tossing them a couple of pieces of fruit from a safe distance. "You're quite the heroes today!"

Momo and Mimi grinned at each other as they enjoyed the fruit. "See, Mimi?" Momo said. "Sometimes playing tricks can lead to good things!"

Mimi laughed, "I guess so, Momo. But let's stick to sunglasses and hats from now on, okay?"

"Deal!" Momo agreed, taking a big bite of his fruit. He looked around at their island home, feeling proud to be a part of it. Every day was an adventure, and he wouldn't have it any other way.

And so, the mischievous monkeys of Monkey Island continued their playful antics, always finding new ways to entertain themselves and their human visitors, while also learning to protect their unique home.

Have fun, but always remember to be kind and considerate to those around you. Respecting nature and its creatures is the best way to enjoy an adventure.

The Great Rabbit Mystery

In the small village of Godalming, nestled in the countryside of England, young Tommy Fletcher sat on a wooden fence, munching on an apple as he watched the townspeople go about their day. It was a peaceful place, usually quiet, with not much happening. But today was different. There was a buzz in the air, a sense of excitement and curiosity that Tommy hadn't felt before.

"Have you heard?" called out his friend, Sally, running up to him with a look of astonishment on her face. "Mary Toft, that lady from the other side of the village, says she's given birth to rabbits!"

Tommy almost choked on his apple. "Rabbits? What do you mean, she gave birth to rabbits?"

"That's what everyone's saying!" Sally replied, wide-eyed. "They say she's had a whole litter of them, and people are coming from all over to see!"

Tommy jumped down from the fence, tossing his apple core into a nearby bush. "I've got to see this with my own eyes. Come on, Sally, let's go!"

The two friends hurried through the cobblestone streets, weaving between carts and passersby until they reached Mary Toft's small cottage. A crowd had already gathered outside, whispering and craning their necks to catch a glimpse of the woman who claimed such an unusual feat.

Inside the cottage, Mary Toft lay on a bed, looking weary but pleased. She was surrounded by curious townsfolk and a few local doctors, all examining the rabbits she had supposedly birthed.

Tommy and Sally squeezed through the crowd and peered inside. Tommy's jaw dropped. "She really did it!" he whispered to Sally. "Look at all those rabbits!"

But Sally wasn't convinced. She crossed her arms and frowned. "It doesn't make any sense, Tommy. How could a person give birth to rabbits? I've never heard of such a thing."

Tommy scratched his head. "Well, I don't know either, but there they are. Maybe it's some kind of miracle?"

Just then, a well-dressed man with a powdered wig and a serious expression pushed his way to the front of the crowd. It was none other than Dr. John Howard, one of the king's own physicians. He had been sent to investigate this strange event.

"Make way, make way!" Dr. Howard commanded, his voice carrying authority. He examined Mary closely and then turned to the crowd. "I need to conduct a thorough investigation. Everyone, please step back!"

The crowd murmured but obeyed, giving Dr. Howard the space he needed. Tommy and Sally, however, stayed close, curious to see what the doctor would do.

Dr. Howard began asking Mary a series of questions. "How did this happen? When did you first feel the rabbits moving inside you? Are there any other animals you've given birth to?"

Mary's answers were vague and inconsistent, but she stuck to her story. "I don't know, sir. It just happened! I was feeling strange, and then out came the rabbits, one after another."

Dr. Howard nodded, his face stern. "Very well. I'll need to take these rabbits back to London for further examination. We must get to the bottom of this."

Over the next few days, the news of Mary Toft's rabbit births spread like wildfire. People came from far and wide to see her and the miraculous rabbits. Some believed it was a sign from God, while others thought it might be a scientific marvel.

Tommy and Sally couldn't stop talking about it. "Do you think it's true?" Sally asked one afternoon as they walked through the village square.

Tommy shrugged. "I don't know. It seems impossible, but everyone's talking about it like it really happened."

Sally nodded. "I've been thinking about it a lot. It just doesn't add up. Maybe there's more to the story than we're being told."

A few days later, Dr. Howard returned to Godalming with another man, Dr. Richard Manningham, a well-known surgeon. They gathered the townspeople and announced that they had conducted a series of tests in London.

"Ladies and gentlemen," Dr. Manningham began, "after a thorough examination, we have determined that this entire affair is a hoax."

A gasp rippled through the crowd. Tommy and Sally exchanged shocked glances.

Dr. Howard continued, "It seems Mary Toft has been placing small rabbits inside herself and then pretending to give birth to them. She did this to gain attention and perhaps receive some kind of reward."

Tommy's eyes widened. "So it was all fake?" he whispered to Sally.

Sally nodded. "I knew something didn't feel right. It just didn't make any sense!"

Mary Toft was brought before the crowd, looking ashamed and embarrassed. "I'm sorry," she said quietly. "I didn't mean to cause so much trouble. I just wanted to make something of myself, to be noticed."

The crowd murmured with mixed emotions—some angry, some amused, others simply relieved that there was a logical explanation.

Dr. Manningham addressed the townsfolk once more. "Let this be a lesson to all. We must always question what we see and hear, especially when it seems too strange to be true. The world is full of wonders, but not all are as they appear."

As the crowd began to disperse, Tommy turned to Sally with a grin. "Well, I guess we learned something today, didn't we?"

Sally smiled back. "Yep. Never believe everything you hear without asking a few questions first."

The two friends laughed and walked away, leaving behind the now quiet cottage of Mary Toft, who had learned her own lesson about honesty and the consequences of deceit.

Always be curious and question things that don't seem right. The truth may not always be obvious, but it's worth finding.

The Great Eiffel Tower Scam

Jacques Dubois was a curious 15-year-old who loved nothing more than to wander the streets of Paris, his home city. One sunny afternoon in 1925, Jacques was riding his bike along the Seine River, his eyes fixed on the towering iron structure that was the pride of Paris: the Eiffel Tower.

As he pedaled closer, Jacques noticed a group of men in suits standing at the base of the tower, gesturing animatedly. Curious, he stopped his bike and leaned in to listen.

"So, you're telling me the city really wants to sell the Eiffel Tower for scrap metal?" one of the men asked, scratching his chin.

"Yes, indeed!" replied a tall man with a slick mustache and a confident smile. "The maintenance costs are too high, and the city needs money. That's where you come in, Mr. Dupont. You have the opportunity to purchase this iconic structure and make a fortune selling the iron!"

Jacques couldn't believe his ears. Sell the Eiffel Tower? That seemed as ridiculous as selling the moon! Jacques decided to follow the man with the mustache, who introduced himself to the others as Monsieur Lustig. He had a feeling something wasn't quite right.

As Jacques trailed behind Lustig and his group, he overheard more of their conversation. Lustig showed the men some official-looking documents, all the while talking about the "secret sale" and how the government wanted to keep the public unaware to avoid an outcry.

Jacques was intrigued and decided to dig deeper into this mystery. He spent the next few days researching this Monsieur Lustig. Through overheard conversations and some quiet snooping around the café Lustig frequented, Jacques discovered that Lustig was known to some people as a con artist. The plot thickened.

He learned that Victor Lustig had recently arrived in Paris and had a reputation for being a smooth talker who could sell anything to anyone. Jacques also found out that the Eiffel Tower was, indeed, expensive to maintain, which gave some credibility to Lustig's story. But still, it seemed absurd to sell such a landmark.

Jacques needed more evidence. He continued to follow Lustig, watching as he met with various scrap metal dealers. It wasn't long before Jacques realized that Lustig wasn't just meeting these men; he was actively convincing them to buy the Eiffel Tower! Lustig played on their ambitions, painting a picture of vast fortunes to be made.

Jacques decided it was time to tell someone who could do something about this. He hurried home and burst through the door, startling his older sister, Marie.

"Marie! You won't believe what I've uncovered!" Jacques panted.

Marie looked up from her book, raising an eyebrow. "What now, Jacques? Another one of your wild stories?"

"No, this is serious!" Jacques insisted. "There's a man trying to sell the Eiffel Tower for scrap metal, and he's already got some businessmen convinced it's a legitimate deal!"

Marie's smile faded as she realized her brother was serious. "Are you sure, Jacques? The Eiffel Tower is a national monument! Who would fall for such a trick?"

Jacques nodded vigorously. "I'm positive. His name is Victor Lustig, and he's already fooled a bunch of them with fake documents and smooth talk."

Marie thought for a moment and said, "If what you're saying is true, we need to go to the police."

The next day, Jacques and Marie made their way to the police station. After convincing a skeptical officer to listen to their story, they were led to Inspector Leclair, a gruff but kind-hearted detective.

"So, you're telling me," Inspector Leclair began, leaning back in his chair, "that someone is trying to sell the Eiffel Tower?"

"Yes!" Jacques exclaimed. "I've seen him with my own eyes. He's tricking businessmen into believing they're buying it for scrap!"

Leclair looked at Jacques and Marie, weighing their words. "Victor Lustig, you say? I've heard of him. A notorious swindler, but selling the Eiffel Tower... that's a new one, even for him."

Inspector Leclair decided to investigate further. He disguised himself as a businessman and arranged a meeting with Lustig at the café Jacques had mentioned. Jacques and Marie, hiding nearby, watched as the inspector approached the con artist.

"Ah, Monsieur Leclair!" Lustig greeted warmly, not suspecting a thing. "Have you come to seize the opportunity of a lifetime?"

Leclair nodded, feigning interest. "Yes, indeed. I'm very interested in this deal."

Lustig launched into his pitch, showing Leclair the same official-looking documents he'd shown the other businessmen. "You see, the Eiffel Tower is a drain on the city's finances. The public doesn't know yet, but soon this iron giant will be sold to the highest bidder for scrap. You could be that bidder."

Leclair played along, nodding and asking questions. "And how do we keep this quiet? Surely the public will notice if the Eiffel Tower starts coming down."

Lustig leaned in, lowering his voice conspiratorially. "Ah, but that's the genius of it! We'll do it piece by piece, under the guise of maintenance work. By the time they realize, it will be too late."

Jacques and Marie, listening in, couldn't help but be impressed by Lustig's nerve. But they also knew it was time to act. They watched as Inspector Leclair signaled to his officers, who were waiting outside.

Suddenly, the café door burst open, and officers swarmed in. "Victor Lustig," Leclair said, standing up and flashing his badge, "you are under arrest for fraud and attempting to deceive these businessmen."

Lustig's face fell, but he quickly regained his composure. "This is an outrage! I demand to speak to my lawyer!"

As the police led Lustig away, Jacques and Marie stepped out of the shadows. Inspector Leclair turned to them with a smile. "Good job, kids. Thanks to you, this scam is over."

Jacques beamed with pride. "I told you it wasn't just a wild story!"

Marie laughed and ruffled her brother's hair. "I guess I should believe you more often, huh?"

Leclair chuckled. "Always trust your instincts, lad. You did good today. Paris is grateful."

As they watched Lustig being taken away, Jacques turned to Marie. "You know, I think I might want to be a detective when I grow up."

Marie smiled. "I think you'd be great at it, Jacques. Just remember to always look for the truth, no matter how strange things might seem."

The siblings walked home together, feeling proud of their adventure. They had learned an important lesson about honesty and the importance of questioning things that didn't seem right. And they couldn't wait to see what mystery they'd uncover next.

In 1925 Victor Lustig succeeded in selling the Eiffel Tower twice. Lustig convinced scrap metal dealers that the French government wanted to secretly sell the iconic structure due to high maintenance costs. Using forged documents and his own powers of persuasion, he conned a dealer out of a large sum of money. Amazingly, Lustig managed to pull off the same scam a second time before fleeing Paris. His audacious deception highlights the importance of skepticism and the need to question deals that seem too good to be true.

Always be curious and skeptical about things that seem too good to be true. Trust your instincts and never be afraid to seek the truth.

Mike, the Miraculous Headless Chicken

Tommy was a curious 11-year-old boy who loved reading about weird and wonderful things. One day, while looking through a book about strange events in history, he came across a story that made him gasp.

"Mama! Mama, come here! You have to see this!" Tommy shouted, waving his mom over to the kitchen table.

"What is it, Tommy?" his mom asked, setting down her laundry basket.

Tommy pointed at the book excitedly. "There was a chicken named Mike who lived without a head for a year and a half! Can you believe that?"

His mom laughed. "A headless chicken? That sounds like one of your funny stories, Tommy."

"No, really!" Tommy insisted. "It happened in a place called Fruita, Colorado, in 1945. A farmer named Lloyd Olsen tried to chop off the chicken's head for dinner, but the chicken didn't die. It just kept walking around like nothing happened!"

His mom sat down, curious now. "Tell me more about this headless chicken, Mike."

Tommy read from the book. "So, the farmer, Mr. Olsen, was shocked when the chicken, Mike, didn't die. Instead of falling over, Mike got up and started pecking at the ground like he still had a head. Can you imagine that?"

His mom shook her head, amazed. "What did the farmer do?"

"Well," Tommy continued, "Mr. Olsen decided to take care of Mike. He fed him with a little dropper, giving him water and small grains of corn. Mike couldn't eat or drink like a normal chicken without a head, so Mr. Olsen had to help him."

"That's incredible," his mom said. "But how could Mike survive without a head? That doesn't make sense."

Tommy grinned. "That's what's so cool about it! The book says that when Mr. Olsen cut off Mike's head, he didn't cut off all of it. Part of Mike's brain stem, the part that controls basic stuff like breathing and heartbeat, was still there. So, Mike could still live and move around, even without most of his head."

His mom's eyes widened. "Wow! I didn't know that was possible. So, what happened next?"

Tommy turned the page. "Mike became famous! People started calling him 'Miracle Mike,' and Mr. Olsen took him on tour around the country. People paid money to see the headless chicken. Mike even got his picture in magazines!"

His mom chuckled. "Imagine paying to see a chicken without a head. What a strange thing!"

"Yeah," Tommy laughed. "But people love strange things. Mike showed how amazing and tough life can be, even when it seems impossible."

"So, did Mike live like that forever?" his mom asked.

Tommy shook his head. "No, he lived for 18 months without his head, which is a really long time for a chicken. One night, while they were on tour, Mike choked on a piece of corn because Mr. Olsen didn't have the dropper with him to help clear Mike's throat. Without it, Mike couldn't breathe, and he passed away."

"That's sad," his mom said softly.

"Yeah, but it's also kind of amazing," Tommy replied. "Mike's story shows how life can be full of surprises. Even when things seem like they should be over, sometimes there's still a chance to keep going, just like Mike did."

His mom smiled and hugged him. "That's a good lesson, Tommy. You never know what you're capable of until you try, even if you're a headless chicken!"

Tommy laughed. "Exactly, Mama! And now I want to learn more about other strange stories in history. Who knows what else I'll find!"

And with that, Tommy grabbed another book from the shelf, ready to discover more amazing tales from history, knowing that sometimes the most unbelievable stories could also be the most inspiring.

Clementine Delake: The Mermaid Girl

I held Dad's hand tightly as we walked through the carnival. There were so many people, so many things to see. The loud music and bright lights made everything feel alive. I could smell popcorn and cotton candy in the air, and I really wanted some, but Dad said we had to hurry.

"Come on, Tommy," Dad said, pulling me along. "There's something special I want to show you."

"What is it?" I asked, trying to keep up with his long strides.

"You'll see," he said with a smile. "It's something you've never seen before."

We walked past all the rides and games, past people shouting and laughing. Then, we reached a big tent with a sign that read: "See the Mermaid Girl! The Marvel of the Century!" Dad paid the man at the entrance, and we went inside.

Inside, it was dark and a little cooler. Posters lined the walls, showing a girl with her legs together like a mermaid. I could hear whispers and murmurs from the crowd, all waiting to see this mermaid girl.

"Is she really a mermaid?" I whispered to Dad.

He chuckled softly. "Not exactly, Tommy. But you'll see."

The man on the stage was tall and had a big voice. "Ladies and gentlemen, gather around! You're about to see something extraordinary, something that will amaze you and touch your hearts. Please welcome Clementine Delake, the Mermaid Girl!"

The curtain opened, and there she was. Clementine was sitting on a chair, smiling gently. Her legs were wrapped in a shiny blue cloth, making her look just like a mermaid. Her eyes were soft and kind, and her smile wasn't like the ones the other performers had. It was real, warm.

I tugged on Dad's sleeve. "She's not a real mermaid, is she?"

"No, Tommy," Dad said quietly. "She's a girl like any other, but with a very special condition."

The man on the stage continued, "Clementine was born with a rare condition called Sirenomelia, or Mermaid Syndrome. It's a condition that caused her legs to be fused together. But despite everything, she's here today to show you her strength and spirit."

Clementine spoke, her voice calm and clear. "I know you came to see something unusual," she began. "But I'm just like you in many ways. I have dreams, hopes, and fears. I've had to face challenges, but they've made me who I am today."

As she spoke, I felt something strange in my chest. I didn't feel sorry for her. She didn't seem like she wanted that. Instead, I felt amazed. She was so brave, standing up there in front of everyone, telling her story.

When I got home, I asked Dad to tell me more about Clementine. He told me she was born in a small town in France in 1892. Her parents were shocked when they saw her legs, and the doctors said she wouldn't survive. But Clementine was strong.

She couldn't walk like other kids, and she spent a lot of time in bed or in a wheelchair. But when she was a teenager, she got a chance to join a traveling circus. At first, her parents didn't want her to go. They were afraid she'd be treated like a spectacle. But Clementine wanted to show people that she was more than just her condition.

"Please let me go," she had begged. "I want to see the world. I want to show people who I really am."

And so, they let her go. She became the "Mermaid Girl," and people from all over came to see her, not just because of her legs but because of her courage. She made friends with other performers who were also different, and they supported each other.

One day after a show, a little girl with crutches approached Clementine and said, "You're so brave. I'm scared to go to school because of how I look, but you make me feel like maybe I can be brave too."

Clementine smiled and held the girl's hand. "It's okay to be scared," she said. "But remember, you are strong, just like me. Don't let anyone make you feel less because you're different."

I thought about that story for a long time. I thought about Clementine and the way she smiled at the crowd. She wasn't just showing them her legs; she was showing them her heart. And I think that's why people came to see her. Not to look at her, but to understand her, to see her strength.

That night, as I lay in bed, I thought about how brave Clementine was. I decided that the next time I felt scared or different, I would remember her words and try to be brave too. Just like the Mermaid Girl.

Conclusion

These stories have shown us that real life can be more incredible and surprising than any fiction. The amazing tales we've explored remind us that the world is full of mysteries waiting to be discovered. Each story in this book reveals that extraordinary events can happen anywhere, at any time, proving that the real world is filled with adventure, wonder, and magic.

Right now, as you read this, new stories are unfolding. Somewhere, someone is making a groundbreaking discovery, overcoming a great challenge, or embarking on an incredible journey that could change the world. Maybe a future genius is just taking their first steps or dreaming big dreams, ready to make a mark on history.

I hope these stories inspire you to see the world differently, to be curious, and to keep asking questions. Remember, the most amazing stories are not just in books—they are happening all around us, every day. Who knows? Maybe one day, your story will be the one that others read and marvel at. So go out, explore, and make your adventure worth telling.

Made in the USA
Las Vegas, NV
07 December 2024

13538655R00044